W9-ADW-816

Life Cycles

Millipedes

by Donna Schaffer

Consultant:
Richard Mankin, Ph.D.
USDA—Agricultural Research Service
Center for Medical, Agricultural,
and Veterinary Entomology

Bridgestone Books
an imprint of Capstone Press
Mankato, Minnesota

8|99

Bridgestone Books are published by Capstone Press
818 North Willow Street, Mankato, Minnesota 56001
http://www.capstone-press.com

Library of Congress Cataloging-in-Publication Data
Schaffer, Donna.
  Millipedes/by Donna Schaffer.
  p. cm.—(Life cycles)
  Includes bibliographical references (p. 23) and index.
  Summary: Describes the physical characteristics, life cycle, behavior, and
adaptations of the millipede.
  ISBN 0-7368-0210-X
  1. Millipedes—Life cycles—Juvenile literature. [1. Millipedes.] I. Title. II. Series:
  Schaffer, Donna. Life cycles.
QL449.6.S36   1999
595.6′6—dc21

                                                                    98-53002
                                                                         CIP
                                                                          AC

Editorial Credits

Christy Steele, editor; Steve Weil/Tandem Design, cover designer; Linda Clavel,
  illustrator; Kimberly Danger, photo researcher

Photo Credits

Bill Beatty, 8, 16
David Liebman, 4, 6
Phillip Roullard, 20-21
Rob Curtis, 18
Robert and Linda Mitchell, 10, 12, 14
Rob and Ann Simpson, cover

Table of Contents

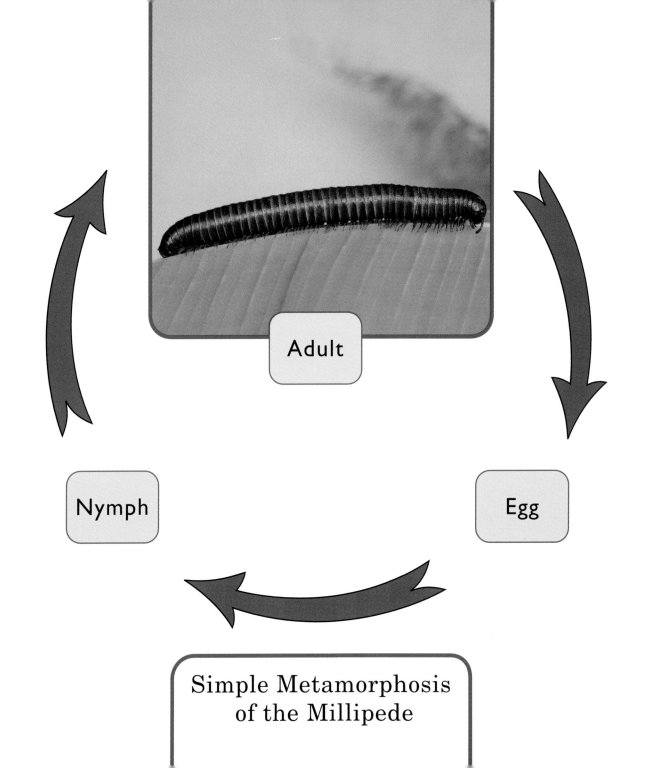

Adult

Nymph

Egg

Simple Metamorphosis
of the Millipede

Life Cycle of the Millipede

Millipedes go through simple metamorphosis. Simple metamorphosis has three stages. A millipede's body form changes during each stage.

Millipedes grow in eggs during the first stage of simple metamorphosis. They look much like adults when they hatch.

Millipedes enter the second life stage after they hatch. Millipedes are called nymphs during this stage. Nymphs are missing some adult body parts. Millipedes grow and develop adult body parts during this stage.

Millipedes enter the adult stage when they are fully grown and have all their body parts. Adult millipedes lay eggs to produce new millipedes. The adult stage is the final stage in a millipede's life.

These three stages make up a millipede's life cycle. Almost all living things go through cycles of birth, growth, reproduction, and death.

The Many-Legged Millipede

About 8,000 different species of millipedes live throughout the world. Each millipede species is different and has its own features. About 1,000 millipede species live in North America.

Millipedes can be many sizes and colors. They range in size from about 1 inch (25 millimeters) to 1 foot (305 millimeters). They can be brown, black, red, or blue.

Many people think millipedes are insects, but they are not. Insects have only three body parts. Millipedes have round bodies made up of many segments. Insects have only six legs. Millipedes may have up to 750 legs.

Millipedes' legs make them part of the animal group Diplopoda. Diplopoda means "double legs." Millipedes have two pairs of legs on most of their body segments.

● ● ● ● **You can see the legs on each of this millipede's ringlike segments.**

Mating Millipedes

Adult millipedes are in the final life stage. They mate to produce more millipedes. Millipedes must mate with others from their own species. But this can be difficult. They first must find others from their species.

Millipedes send out pheromones to show they are ready to mate. These scents help males and females of the same species find each other.

Males also may rub their legs together to make sounds. The sound is called stridulation. Stridulation attracts females. Male millipedes then use their antennas and legs to touch females gently.

These millipedes are mating.

The Life Cycle Begins

After mating, female millipedes build nests. Females of most species build nests underground. Some make nests out of their waste matter.

Females lay eggs in spring or in warm weather. They lay groups of sticky eggs in their nests. The egg is the first life stage of a millipede.

Females from different species lay different numbers of eggs. Females from some species lay up to 2,000 eggs. Healthy females lay more eggs than sick females.

Some female millipedes wrap their bodies around their eggs. This process is called brooding. Brooding keeps the eggs warm and safe.

The eggs hatch in about three weeks. The second stage of a millipede's life then begins.

● ● ● ● **This female is brooding.**

Young Millipedes

Young millipedes look like small adult millipedes. But they grow and change throughout the second life stage.

Millipedes have a hard outer covering called an exoskeleton. Millipedes must shed their exoskeleton to let their bodies grow. They usually go through this molting process seven to 10 times before becoming adults.

After hatching, most young millipedes have only three pairs of legs. Millipedes grow legs and body segments during each molt. The number of body parts added depends on the kind of millipede.

● **These young millipedes look like adult millipedes. But they are lighter in color and have fewer segments than adults.**

A Molting Chamber

Nests are not just places for eggs to hatch. Nests also are good places for millipedes to keep cool and moist. Millipedes lose body moisture in hot, dry weather. Millipedes die if they become too dry.

Nests also protect millipedes when they molt. Millipedes stay in one spot as they molt. During this time, they are weak and unable to defend themselves. Animals can catch millipedes easily when they are molting.

The number of times millipedes molt varies. But millipedes generally spend more than one-tenth of their lives molting. Millipedes usually stop molting when they reach adulthood.

Many species of millipedes become adults after one year. Other species may take four or five years.

● ● ● ● **This blue cloud-forest millipede is making a nest from its waste matter.**

Millipede Survival

Millipedes from some species live up to 13 years. All millipedes need certain conditions to survive.

Climate is an important element in the survival of millipedes. Millipedes breathe through spiracles along the sides of their bodies. These tiny holes stay open. Too much heat passing through the spiracles is dangerous. Millipedes could dry out and die. So they make nests or seek out dark, moist places. Millipedes often live deep in the soil or under stones or logs.

Millipedes must live near food. They eat dead plants and leaves. Eating this food also is important to the environment. Millipedes help break down dead plants and leaves into soil. This process helps new plants grow.

● ● ● ● **Millipedes stay in nests to keep moist.**

Predators

Millipedes have many predators. Birds, frogs, lizards, and scorpions eat millipedes. Millipedes have hard exoskeletons that protect them. But their undersides are soft. Predators attack the soft undersides of millipedes.

Millipedes protect themselves in several ways. They roll their bodies to hide their soft underbellies. Predators may have a hard time breaking through the exoskeleton.

Millipedes' glands also protect them. These body parts ooze a bad-smelling liquid when enemies attack. The smell usually is enough to stop predators. Some millipedes release a liquid that is poisonous to other animals.

The habits of millipedes keep them safe. Millipedes usually hide during the day and come out only at night. Darkness makes it hard for predators to see millipedes.

This millipede has rolled its body into a ball to protect its soft underside from predators.

Adaptation

Millipedes' bodies have developed features that make living in different places possible.

For example, this greenhouse millipede lives in gardens. A greenhouse millipede's body shape helps it burrow into soil. The greenhouse millipede even eats soil. Strong mouthparts help it crunch the soil into smaller pieces.

Millipedes use their many legs to push themselves through soil and dead leaves. The pairs of legs work together to give millipedes more power.

You can see this greenhouse millipede's sensing antennas. Millipedes cannot see well. They have adapted by using their antennas to help them move around.

Hands On: Millipedes and Moisture

Millipedes need moist conditions to survive. You can do this experiment to see how millipedes seek moisture.

What You Need

Two empty shoeboxes   Warm water
One large box   One thin towel
One empty plastic container   Three or four millipedes

What You Do

1. Put the two shoeboxes inside the large box.
2. Fill the plastic container with warm water.
3. Put the container in one of the shoeboxes.
4. Place the towel over both shoeboxes.
5. Place the millipedes on the towel where it covers the shoebox without water.
6. Watch to see what the millipedes do.

Where do they go? The millipedes will smell the moisture from the water. They will move across the towel to the other shoebox.

Words to Know

antennas (an-TEN-uhs)—feelers on the heads of some animals

brood (BROOD)—to protect eggs until they hatch

exoskeleton (eks-oh-SKEL-uh-tuhn)—a hard covering on the outside of millipedes

molt (MOHLT)—to shed an outer skin

pheromones (FER-uh-mohnz)—special scents that animals send to signal that they are ready to mate

spiracles (SPEER-uh-kuhlss)—tiny holes through which some animals breathe

stridulation (strih-juh-LAY-shuhn)—the sound millipedes make by rubbing their legs together; male millipedes rub their legs together to attract mates.

Read More

Landau, Elaine. *Minibeasts as Pets.* New York: Children's Press, 1997.

Watts, Barrie. *Wood Lice and Millipedes.* Keeping Minibeasts. New York: Franklin Watts, 1991.

Useful Addresses

Department of Entomology
Royal Ontario Museum
Toronto, ON M5S 2C6
Canada

**Young Entomologists'
 Society**
6907 West Grand River
 Avenue
Lansing, MI 48906

Internet Sites

Introduction to Millipedes
http://kalypso.cybercom.net/~dhe/Meadow/
 IntroMill.html

Millipede
http://www.pma.edmonton.ab.ca/natural/insects/
 projects/milliped.htm

Index

DATE			